W9-BEG-261

BUILDING HAPPY MEMORIES
AND
FAMILY TRADITIONS

BY Verna Birkey
You Are Very Special

COMPILED BY Verna Birkey and Jeanette Turnquist
A Mother's Problem Solver

*Building Happy Memories
and Family Traditions*

Building Happy Memories

and

Family Traditions

COMPILED BY *Verna Birkey*

AND *Jeanette Turnquist*

FLEMING H. REVELL COMPANY
Old Tappan, New Jersey

Unless otherwise identified, Scripture quotations in this volume are from the King James Version of the Bible.

Scripture quotations identified NIV are from HOLY BIBLE New International Version, copyright ©, New York International Bible Society, 1978. Used by permission.

Scripture quotations identified NAS are from the New American Standard Bible, Copyright © THE LOCKMAN FOUNDATION 1960, 1962, 1963, 1968, 1971, 1972, 1973, 1975 and are used by permission.

For information on the Enriched Living Workshops taught by Verna Birkey, write: Seminar Workshops for Women, P.O. Box 3039, Kent, WA 98031.

Library of Congress Cataloging in Publication Data

Birkey, Verna.
    Building happy memories and family traditions.

    1. Family—Religious life.   2. Birkey, Verna.   I. Turnquist, Jeanette, joint author.   II. Title.
BV4526.2.B57   248.4   80-15911
ISBN 0-8007-1126-2

This book is dedicated to the Enriched Living
Workshop alumnae who have shared happy
memories from their childhood days, as well
as the new memories they are now building into
the lives of their own children; and to all
whose lives will be enriched through this little
volume of practical memory-building helps.

Contents

Introduction

"I remember . . . it was during the depression years of the thirties. Our family didn't have much money at all. Dimes were precious items, but my father had given me one to go swimming. I was so happy! I knew it was a sacrifice. On my way to the pool, I lost the dime. Sad and crying, I started back home: no dime, no swimming. Just then, my father, who was a traveling salesman, came by, listened to my story, was touched by my feelings, and reached deep into his pocket to replace my lost dime. I remember he spoke so kindly as he dried my tears."

My friend's story goes back four decades, but the precious memory is preserved in her adult mind, and the recall of it warms her heart with the knowledge, "I was loved!"

Everyone needs a storehouse of precious memories that enhance a sense of belonging, a sense of being loved, a sense of worth, a sense of competence. A memory becomes valuable as it relates to one's needs being met. The opposite is also true—unpleasant memories are the product of situations when one's basic needs were not being met.

Parents, teachers, friends, sisters, aunts, uncles, and grandparents have the joyous privilege of helping children, young people, and other adults build happy memories that can feed their souls' needs. This can be an instrument for developing a whole person, building character, and reproducing happy memories in others.

A memory is a legacy—something special, handed down from one generation to another. It can be much more than a material object. In fact, the best memories are often stored only in the mind, not in the cedar chest or the far corner of the attic.

Family togetherness is a memory. Sometimes it involves doing the same thing in the same way enough times, until it becomes a tradition. "That's the way we do it at our house. It's always been that way. That's what makes birthdays special!" "It wouldn't be Christmas without it." Sometimes it's a surprise that will never be forgotten, but probably never repeated. Sometimes it's, "That's just the way my mother was!"

Building Happy Memories and Family Traditions gives you a library of ideas from which you can choose some "memories" that you would like to leave as a legacy to those dear to you. There are small ideas and big ideas. There are activities that will become treasured traditions on Christmas, birthdays, and Thanksgiving. There are once-in-a-lifetime memories. But most of all, there are the small, daily acts of kindness that we treasure most.

Here is a wealth of ideas and idea stimulators. As you read, you will also find yourself remembering and defining your best memories. Perhaps there will be choice ones from your childhood that you will begin to implement now, in your own home. Make it your aim to leave many happy memories with those around you. After all, a memory is a simple act of love, and isn't that what a family is all about?

BUILDING HAPPY MEMORIES
AND
FAMILY TRADITIONS

PART 1

HOW WE CELEBRATED
SPECIAL DAYS

1

Warm Christmas Traditions

And she shall bring forth a son, and thou shalt call his name Jesus: for he shall save his people from their sins.

Matthew 1:21

The Twelve Days of Christmas

When our three children were very young, we established a tradition for the twelve days before Christmas. We drew names and kept the name we drew a secret. During those twelve days, we went out of our way to be especially kind to that person. We would often find a kind note or a piece of gum, or other small gift, on our pillow. We also established the habit of sharing helpful Scripture verses in our notes.

On Christmas Eve, we would each try to guess who had our name. If many people voted for you, this meant you had been especially kind to other members of the family. On Christmas Eve, we would reveal our names with a small gift for that person. Our children are now in their late teens and still look forward to this tradition.

Christmas Cards at Prayer

After Christmas, we saved all our Christmas cards and put them in a basket. Each evening before dinner, we drew

15

out one card, reread it, and then each of us offered prayer for the person or family that sent the card. How precious it was, to hear our four-year-old praying that her friend's Daddy might ask Jesus into his heart. This has increased our appreciation and our thanks to God for our precious friends and family. It has also been a time of sharing our past with the children. "Janie was my college roommate," I would explain. Then I would share something special about Janie.

This project lasted until the middle of March. Each evening I would write a short note, telling the person we had prayed for him or her that day. We received several responses saying what an encouragement it had been to receive the note during times of difficult circumstance in their lives. The children wait in expectation of what God will do in each family. When the cards were all drawn, the children asked if we could start over again.

Christmas Windowsills

We live in an old farmhouse with extremely wide windowsills. At Christmastime, our four children draw numbers to choose which windowsill they will decorate. This has been a traditional family project for twenty-five years. Now the grandchildren are starting to participate. Decoration must be finished by December 10. Judging is done by the entire family, and prizes are awarded. This has taught them to demonstrate the real meaning of Christmas, and we, as parents, know where they are in their understanding of Christmas, since they discuss their plans with us.

Christmas Witness

To try to put the emphasis of the Christmas season in proper perspective for our four children, ages sixteen, fifteen, twelve, and eight, the week before Christmas, we devote one evening to each child. He can invite a friend for dinner or dessert. We plan songs, games, some pertinent Scripture, and a time for total family fellowship. As the children have many unsaved friends, this is a time when we can all share the real meaning of Christmas with them in an atmosphere of love. Then, the following week, we concentrate our family prayer time on these friends, praying that they will come to know Christ as their Savior.

Twenty-five Days of Christmas

We have two children, three and four years old. Time is difficult for them to understand, so it's hard to look forward to a Saturday picnic, a birthday, or Christmas. Last Christmas we began a family project to cover the first twenty-five days of December. We called it our Advent Chain. There are twenty-five paper loops. The girls took turns removing a loop every morning, to see what we do that day.

Some days listed traditional Christmas necessities: Buy the tree with Daddy after dinner; decorate the tree tonight; wrap Daddy's gifts today; shop for a gift for Grandma and Grandpa. Most of the days, however, the activities were deeds of kindness, to show our love and concern to others: Bake cookies; take cookies to any friend you choose; pray for the sick people who won't be home for Christmas; build fire in fireplace, make popcorn, and invite the neighbors over to sing Christmas carols; call cousin Doug (long-distance) to wish him a Merry Christmas.

This was so enjoyed by our girls that we now make a monthly calendar on the wall, with pictures of what's going to happen that month. (We want to keep the chain idea special for Christmas.) The picture calendar helps them anticipate weekends and events during the week, and it helps me to think of creative, fun things for them during the week (Go to the library for an hour; meet Daddy for lunch at the park) to break up the wait for Saturday and Sunday fun times.

Serving Each Other

In our large family, we draw names for gifts at Christmas. The cards we draw also include a special prayer request and a special service that we would appreciate being given consistently during Advent. For instance, my husband got our oldest girl's name, and he was requested to help her make her bed for five days. I drew one son's name, and he wanted someone to take bike rides with regularly. We each learned that we have a need to serve each other individually.

Personalized Ornaments

In an attempt to establish some family traditions when our children were young, we began giving each one an ornament for the Christmas tree every year. We write the year and the child's name or initials on it. It has become a special project for Dad and Mom to plan each year. These are not ordinary glittering baubles; they are personalized to suit the individual child's interests and personality. Last year, Jackie's was an interesting combination of cloth, tape measure, pins, and all that goes with learning to sew. Ben's was a toy trumpet, to commemorate his year of faithful practice and improvement.

They each put theirs away, after Christmas, in a special box with their name on it. As they have grown older, they have appreciated this more and more. They connect special memories with each year's ornaments, as they add them all to the tree. When they leave home, they will take their collections with them, to begin their own trees.

Christmas Thankfulness

In our family, we developed a special custom for Christmas Eve. With a desire to honor the Christ of Christmas and build in our children a spirit of thankfulness and appreciation for each gift received, when the children were tiny, we began the custom of sitting around the Christmas tree, all holding hands. Each one prays, remembering God's gift to us in the gift of His Son and praying for those who brought gifts to us and for those receiving gifts from us. This sets the tone and takes the frantic excitement out of tearing into the gifts. Each card is read, and gifts are opened one at a time. This taught appreciation of both the gift and the giver. Our children still practice this custom in their own homes.

A Family Tree

Through the years we have established a family Christmas tree. Every Christmas a new ornament, containing the child's picture, is added to the tree. This year our son will have nineteen and our daughter fourteen! It has become a conversation piece, and our children are so proud of it. Needless to say, it's also a special time of reminiscing for parents! This year our nineteen-year-old son wants his picture on top of the tree. Guess where his picture is going to be? You're right: on top of the tree!

Annual Christmas-Tree-Cutting Trip

Eighteen years ago we started taking an annual Christmas-tree-cutting trip—our four children and Dad and I. This December there were twelve of us. We have doubled in number, with the addition of two sons-in-law and two girl friends and two grandsons. We all look for the right tree, cut it down together, and then go have a big Italian dinner together. My children loved running through the trees, and this year our grandsons took the place of our boys, running through the trees. It's a great together time for the family.

Celebrating Jesus' Birthday

Our family is grown, and our children have families of their own. They usually come together at our home for several days each Christmas. To make our Christmas together the celebration of Jesus' birthday, instead of only a time of giving and receiving, I wrote to our daughter and son-in-law and our son and daughter-in-law, asking them to be thinking of fun, family things we could do together. They were each to be responsible for one activity and one dinner, and we would all cooperate. The Christmas Eve dinner and evening activity was reserved for my husband and me. They loved it.

There was no TV for two full days. We watched home movies from their childhood, had a weiner roast, ice-skated, and so forth. After dinner on Christmas Eve, we gathered in the living room, where I told them a Christmas story. Then Bill read them *the* Christmas story from Luke, which was followed by prayer. We continued to celebrate Christ's birthday as we handed out gifts. The evening was complete when we went to the candlelight communion service at church, our hearts truly prepared. They eagerly look forward to this each year, and now they don't talk about the things they *received,* but rather what we *did.*

Christmas Tradition

By candlelight on Christmas Eve, we, as a family, read the Christmas story, sing several carols, have prayer, and then open our gifts. We started this when the children were tiny, and it has now become a tradition. Our children are now eighteen, seventeen, and twelve years old. When they were younger, there was quite a difference in their understanding of the Christmas story, so we would read for the youngest level and sing songs to the older level. Though they have many of their own activities now, all of them still want to continue our tradition.

Christmas Servants

Every Christmas, rather than giving only material gifts, we also give Service Cards. This brings us Christmas all year.

> This card entitles you, Mom, to a Saturday morning's help with anything you want done.
> This card entitles you, Dad, to my help for a day at the office, weeding out your files, and so forth.
> This card entitles you, Johnny, to suggest any family activity you'd like us to do together.
> This card, Liz, entitles you to my help with any sewing project you have in mind.
> This card entitles you, Dad, to my help in cleaning out the garage or digging your garden spot.

Sometimes the card offers an activity we know the other person would like to do:

> This card entitles you, Johnny, to three free games of racketball with me.
> This card, Tommy, entitles you to an evening at miniature golf.

The response has always been good—especially from busy Mom and Dad. We would both rather have a Service Card than anything purchased! Usually, after all the clutter is cleared away, one of the children will throw his arms around us and exclaim, "This is the neatest Christmas, and the Service Cards are the best of all. Thank you!"

A Love Gift

I give each one in my family a Love Gift at Christmastime. After carefully listening to my husband and two boys (fourteen and seventeen), I determine what my Love Gift to each should be. It may not be a big thing: One was to change the sheets each week for a year, on the youngest one's bed. But as I carry out my gift of love through that year, it brings me closer to that member of the family. As I do it, the Lord gives me such joy and blessing and puts a prayer in my heart for that one, as I'm giving his gift of love. I am learning that as I take on a servant's attitude, this is freeing them to give of themselves in areas that were battlegrounds before.

Christmas Thanksgiving

At Christmastime we have a Tree of Thanksgiving. At Thanksgiving I pick a small branch off a tree and mount it. Then each day between Thanksgiving and Christmas, we write a thank-you for something that day. I make up colored papers in shapes of bells, snowmen, and stars for each thank-you. We have great fun with this, and it has become a traditional Christmas activity for our family.

Jesus' Birthday

At Christmas we wanted to emphasize Jesus' birthday and the spirit of giving to our small son, Adam. He helped me wrap a shoe box with foil and put a bow on it, to make it look like a Christmas package. Then we cut a hole, to make a bank. Adam told anyone who asked (and some who didn't) that it was his birthday present to Jesus. He voluntarily gave up all extra goodies from the grocery store during December and put the money in his special bank. Mama and Daddy gave up their treats, too, to add to the gift. At Christmas we sent the money to some missionary friends in the Ivory Coast. You should see the expressions of bank employees and post-office personnel, when a little boy comes in with this special bank! He was able to tell them all about what he was doing.

The final treat was the letter Adam received from his friends in the Ivory Coast. They printed it, so he could read some words. The letter said that they used the money to buy Bibles for their junior-high class. Adam is so pleased to know that he helped other children learn about Jesus.

Christmas Secrets

As a teacher, I am responsible for developing a warm and contented climate in my classroom. One way we do this at Christmastime is to have secret class pals. Each day of the week before Christmas, we are to either write a note, telling about a nice thing the secret pal has done, or give a little gift (an apple, a picture, a card) to our secret pal. The day before Christmas vacation, we bring a small gift with our name written inside, to reveal our identity to our secret pal.

Music Appreciation

Around Christmastime, we take our four children (all under twelve) into Seattle to hear the *Messiah* or some other well-known Christmas music. This has increased their interest and appreciation of good music and has been an occasion they really look forward to. It's surprising how they will recognize a famous aria or chorus, such as the "Hallelujah Chorus," when they hear it sung later.

2

My Birthday Was Uniquely My Day

For you created my inmost being; you knit me together in my mother's womb. I praise you because I am fearfully and wonderfully made; your works are wonderful, I know that full well.
Psalms 139:13, 14 NIV

Birthday Tiara

We didn't realize until recently that what we did to honor the birthday child in our home was a big thing for our daughters (now twenty and twenty-three). When they were young, we had a jeweled tiara (crown), which they wore all day on their birthday. Also, they didn't have to do any work on their birthday, and I put out the flag for their day, just as we do for presidents' birthdays. As they reminisced at their last birthday dinner, I realized that this made them feel a very special and loved member of the family.

Teenage Celebration

Our children are all over twenty years old now. Since they were teenagers, in addition to celebrating on their day, we have celebrated all of our birthdays together, by spending a night or a weekend together at a motel. The children loved the swimming pool and the game room, and being together brought much harmony to our family. One person was honored at each meal. It was always a fantastic time!

Tenth Birthday With Daddy

On each child's tenth birthday, he or she had a special day alone with Daddy. With some guidelines as to cost and distance, they could choose what they would like to do with their daddy for one whole day. Since my husband travels a great deal and is gone quite a bit, this has offered both children an opportunity to feel special and to get better acquainted with their dad. Their tenth birthdays have now come and gone, so we periodically announce that one of the children will have another special day with Dad. Last year, our son chose to go fishing. As we eat the fish that we put in the freezer when they returned, Keith is again reminded of and relives his fishing day with Dad. This has been a very positive thing in building relationships and happy memories in our family.

A Song at 11:46 P.M.

"Born to the proud parents John and Mary Smith, a beautiful baby girl *on February 21, 1949, at 11:46 P.M.!*"

Every year that I can remember, my mom and dad have sung "Happy Birthday" to me at exactly *11:46 P.M. every February 21*. They used to wake me up in the night to sing to me. Even after I was married, they phoned me at 11:46 P.M. from New Mexico. They never wait to hear me say hello. As soon as I pick up the phone, the song begins! This year I was not at home at the familiar hour, and I phoned them at 11:46 P.M. Sure enough, they didn't even say hello, the song just began. It made my traumatic thirtieth birthday a lot more fun! What's more, I had been sick all week and feeling low. This tradition has really made me feel that they are glad I entered their family that night.

Love Notes for Daddy

Daddy's birthday was close at hand, and money was short. We (our three children, seven, five, and one years, and I) were busy making a cake with a special design on top, but the children were concerned about giving a gift, too. On strips of paper, we wrote special things we would do for Daddy or wanted to say to Daddy.

- Good for a bike ride with Kent.
- Good for a kiss from Mom.
- Good for help with the lawn from Cathy.
- Good for a quiet time reading your magazines.
- Good for some mending of your clothes.
- I love you, Daddy.

The children were excited as we folded the papers and put them in a pretty vase. When Daddy opened his gift, he read aloud every one of the love notes. "Oh, this is a good one!" was his reply, making each person feel special. The kids were delighted, and Mom had tears of joy! The vase had a special place of honor on Daddy's dresser, and he cashed in the love notes as the year went on, so it was a continuing gift.

Limericks in Rhyme

When our children were small and we had very little money, we still wanted each child's birthday to be very special. In order to make the day one to look forward to, we began hiding our small gifts and writing notes containing clues on how to find them; the clues became harder as the children grew. Then my husband, who's able to do a lot with rhyming words, began writing what we called Limericks in Rhyme with the clues. We began this practice when the children were five and continued until they were fifteen. Each child made mention on his seventeenth birthday that birthdays weren't as fun as they used to be, since we had gotten away from this tradition. They are grown now and often tell how special this was and how much more fun it made birthdays. Both children tell us they plan to do this in their own families, when they have them.

Half-Birthdays

We celebrate half-birthdays as well as birthdays. In the month of the child's birthday, he can choose where he would like to spend the entire day with his father. Since we have only two children, this gives me a day alone with the other child. In the month of the half-birthday, the child gets an evening out with his father, while the other one and I spend the evening together at home, doing something special. This is special to the children. They look forward to it and plan for weeks ahead where they would like to go with Dad.

A Kiss or a Kind Word

Each birthday, before the birthday child awakens, the rest of the family (seven of us) gather together, to the birthday child's room, and awaken him with the happy birthday song. Later in the day, when we are having the cake and presents, we each go up (starting with the youngest child), shake hands or kiss or say something kind to the birthday child. Sometimes one remarks, "Oh, do we *have* to do this again?" But if the time is growing late and we haven't done it yet, we are always eagerly reminded, "It's time to go, one by one."

When I'm Ten!

For each child's tenth birthday, we take the child on a vacation planned for and by the ten-year-old. It's a week to ten days when the child has Mom and Dad to himself. When we return home, we compile a book of photos and mementos of "Todd's vacation." They enjoy recalling their experience with their brother and sister and friends. This also builds great interest and anticipation for "When I'm ten!" from the younger children. God has used this time to bind us together and prepare us all for maintaining closeness during the challenging teen years. It's also a joy to see the children rejoice with one another in this special time.

Unbirthday Party

My mother's birthday is on Christmas, so I give her an Unbirthday Party in the summer. She's always surprised. It's a typical birthday party, with cake, ice cream, streamers, balloons, and one unique present with a homemade card. We hear so much about doing things for the children that families forget that grandparents, aunts, and uncles like surprises and presents for no particular reason, too! This Unbirthday Party greatly cements our relationship. It has become a regular part of our summer, though Mother never knows the day it will be. She loves it!

Chocolate Cake and Car Keys

To celebrate our son's sixteenth birthday, I baked his favorite chocolate cake. Then I decided to make it more personal by decorating it with a little toy car and a set of car keys, in recognition of this exciting time of life for a boy beginning to drive.

Birthday Cup

Birthdays are special times, and I'm glad I can remember that my parents made mine very special. When I was a child, we had a special cup that was only used on birthdays by the birthday person.

3

Our Way of Thanksgiving

Give thanks to the Lord, for He is good; For His lovingkindness is everlasting.

Psalms 136:1 NAS

Thanksgiving Harmony

For Thanksgiving, we had twenty-one members of our family together. With this many temperaments and personalities, there can be some small areas of conflict. So, to promote family harmony, after dinner we passed around a piece of paper to each person, children included. The name of one person was at the bottom. We then asked everyone to write one word, describing a character trait or quality that they enjoyed or appreciated about the person whose name was at the bottom of the paper. After he wrote his word at the top of the paper, he folded the paper so no one could see it and passed it on to the next person, who added his word and folded the paper. There was a lot of giggling and laughing—it's very hard for my family to be serious! We then gave each person the paper with his name on it. These turned out to be "warm fuzzies."

It was interesting to notice the eagerness of some of the teenagers, as they read their list of warm fuzzies. Others acted very cool about it all. It was rewarding to spend time thinking positive thoughts about our loved ones. Philippians 4:8: "... whatsoever things are true ... honest ... just ... pure ... lovely ... of good report ... think on these things."

Thanksgiving Around a Bonfire

My childhood Thanksgiving Days were most unconventional. We had no turkey, stuffing, and cranberries, nor was our celebration around a table inside a warm house. Each year, several families went together on a picnic at the unpopulated seashore. We built a bonfire, brought baskets of goodies and equipment for games, such as a football, a badminton set, and hiking shoes.

With children of all sizes and shapes, there were activities for everyone. The fathers and big boys did the cooking of hamburgers or seafood over the open fire, while the salads and fruits and cakes were lovingly prepared at home earlier, by the women.

Since we lived in North Carolina, it was often a balmy day of extended fall temperatures or sometimes a cold, crisp day of early winter. After a day in God's beautiful world, surrounded by the wonders of nature, everyone came home truly thankful for love, fellowship, good friends, family, God, and His creation.

Turkey Verses

Several years ago, one of our sons created what proved to be an enduring Thanksgiving tradition. While he made Pilgrim place cards for our Thanksgiving table, I made brown-paper turkeys that had a slit which held a promise card.

Every year, I've asked God to guide us as to which Scripture would go at each place. After dinner, each person, including guests, would read the verse on their "turkey."

This year, as we pulled out the now slightly dog-eared turkeys, I noticed the Scripture still on our twenty-year-old's marker from last year and could hardly keep back the tears for the praise that filled my heart. Last year he was not really following the Lord. His verse was, "In all thy ways acknowledge him, and he shall direct thy paths" (Proverbs 3:6). During this year, he has come to the place of acknowledging Jesus Christ as Lord and is in Bible college, happy with God's leading in his life.

This year I struggled a bit about putting the turkeys and verses on our table. Two of our sons are trying very hard to leave God out of their lives. Not knowing what their reaction would be to our traditional custom, we prayed and committed the situation to the Lord. We wondered if they would excuse themselves and leave before we finished with our meal, but they did stay, and they read their Scripture. We had chosen verses that reminded them of God's love and desires for them. It turned out that these verses were "just for them!" We rejoice, for God has promised that His Word will not return void.

Thanksgiving Hideaway

Our family is grown, and now live in nearby towns. All agreed it would be fun to have a special time each year, when we could count on being together to share and enjoy one another. Our solution was to rent a cabin in the mountains for four days over Thanksgiving. The cabin is only two hours from home but away from TV, telephones, jobs, and other interruptions.

Our emphasis each year is on our thankfulness to God for our blessings. Each family brought its own bedding and supplied meals for one day, as well as part of the festive meal. In addition, each family planned a family sharing time for the day, based on the Thanksgiving theme—including Scripture, songs, and testimonies. They also brought an idea and supplies to share for Christmas decorations to be made by all in the evening. This has really cemented our family as it increases in number, and it gives us something special to look forward to each fall.

Over the River . . . .

Since we are a military family, we have been separated from our "larger" family on most of the holiday occasions for togetherness. One way we planned to be with the grandparents when the rest of the family was also there was by making a family tape and sending it in time to be shared on Thanksgiving. We wanted it to be special and fun, so we rehearsed and planned very carefully. We began with our family musical group, consisting of Mother on organ, oldest son on guitar, daughter and youngest son clapping and singing, Daddy encouraging, "All together now, 'Over the river and through the woods, to Grandfather's house we go.' " Following the musical introduction, amid much giggling, each one greeted the family separately. Then followed some family chatting and reminders to exchange names for

Christmas, thank-yous for letters and gifts through the year, and so forth.

We anticipated their reactions and laughed happily over the thought of each person's response, making a great deal of fun for ourselves on a Sunday afternoon.

4

We Celebrated Everything

A cheerful heart is good medicine, but a crushed spirit dries up the bones.

Proverbs 17:22 NIV

Celebrating Everything!

We celebrate everything. When six-year-old Elizabeth broke her leg, she received the support of friends and family to encourage her. But, as those weeks in a cast seemed to grow longer and longer, we planned a Cast Off party, complete with decorations, sign on the door, homemade cards, refreshments, and grandparents. She helped to plan the celebration and make the decorations, so the anticipation turned something difficult into a positive time of joy.

I Did it Because I Love You

At our house we have a little sign, hastily made one Valentine's Day and now rather dingy and battered, which says:

This note has shown up in expected places, and at unexpected times, next to:

- A stack of voluntarily washed dishes
- A bed left unmade, but now neatly made
- A sparkling clean bathroom
- A breakfast table, beautifully and quietly set while the rest of the family still slept

Happy Tooth-Out

We celebrate Tooth Days. Each child gets to be the "Tooth Fairy" for another child—picking out a new book to be slipped under the pillow at night. We have special refreshments, such as tooth-shaped cakes, and a special "Happy Tooth-Out" song at dinner that night.

Summer Coupons

On Memorial Day each year, just before school is out, I give each of our six children a Coupon Special. My purpose is to try to meet the special, individual desires we can't meet as a group. One daughter wanted time alone, to go to the tide pools at Hood Canal. Another wanted time to go to the river for lunch. One son wanted a special trip to the library, with no rush to get books and run. This system provides six coupons and six chances for me to be alone with a child. It works great for building relationships. Now everyone eagerly looks forward to May 30, for the beginning of fun times with Mom.

Family Anniversary

My husband and I had always felt our wedding anniversary was just for the two of us, but one year, we decided to celebrate at home with the kids. I fixed steak and all the trimmings and set the table with candles and china. When they came into the room, they were all eyes, seeing how special everything looked. They used their company manners and were really impressed with the occasion. Many times since then, they have commented about our candlelight dinner. I'm glad we shared "our time" and really made it "ours" that year.

A Baked Valentine

On Valentine's Day I bake a cake and put little notes in it. The children love it and look forward to it every year. I bake a heart-shaped cake or cupcakes, write some love notes, positive messages, or short Bible verses on strips of paper, fold the papers in small squares, wrap them in foil, and place the notes throughout the cake batter. When the children get a piece of cake, they love to check to see if there's a note in their piece. The notes can just be a simple "I love you" or anything your imagination comes up with.

April Fool's Day Surprise

I always put an April Fool surprise in my husband's lunch box on April 1. When our first child started school, he wanted to be sure I would pack his lunch on April 1, instead of his buying a lunch. I knew he was hoping I would do some of the same special surprises I had done with his daddy. When he was in first grade, I packed his lunch on April 1. Instead of the usual one sandwich, I put in two. The top one had cardboard between a buttered roll; the next one was his favorite baloney. He was delighted that I also remembered him with a little amusing trick. He confessed that evening that he had checked his lunch box as soon as he had gotten on the bus. Just the other day he was checking the calendar and, with disappointment in his voice, said, "Oh my! April first comes on Saturday this year!"

Monthly Anniversaries

My husband and I go out for a special evening each month on the date of our anniversary. That evening, we share with each other either something we feel would help our mate to grow or some small habit or kindness which we would like him or her to practice that month. Then, on the following month's date, we report to each other. We both have found it a time in which we can share very openly and honestly some weakness of the other which may, in fact, be a blind spot. For example, my husband said he would appreciate having the porch light on, when he comes home. I told him I would like to see his smile in the mornings.

We were delighted to work on these little things, and now they have become habits. It has been exciting to look back in the notebook we made of these monthly activities, to see how many changes have become permanent ones as we desire to please each other and the Lord.

Mother's Day Car Picnic

On Mother's Day, my children like to do something special for me. Since May is a rainy season in our area, they prepare a lunch and we have a car picnic. We drive to the top of a nearby mountain. Sometimes it stops raining long enough for us to get out and look at the view and walk around a little. Then we go to the car, spread out our lunch, and have a fun time eating and laughing. We have a few minor spills, but Mother's Day is very special because of our car picnic.

Valentines by Candlelight

My husband is a pastor, and we have five lovely daughters, ages seventeen, fourteen, thirteen, eleven, and eight. Valentine's Day has come to be a very special day at our house. We cancel everything. I cook a company meal. We eat on the good china by candlelight in the dining room. Each year I plan a different dessert—heart-shaped cookies with their names on them, a heart-shaped cake exclaiming, "We love you all." We get each of our girls a carefully chosen card. My husband helps me prepare dinner while the girls are locked out, then he leads them into the dining room with their eyes closed, while I stand with the camera ready. They love it! Oh yes—the phone is off the hook. It is a night when we tell them how neat and special they are to us. They really look forward to it.

PART 2

HOW WE SHARED
HAPPY TIMES OF
FAMILY TOGETHERNESS

5

Fun and Surprises

. . . the cheerful heart has a continual feast.

Proverbs 15:15 NIV

Rainy Day at Grandpa's

Being reared on a farm in postdepression days, our pleasures and extracurricular activities as a family were minimal. But one thing stands out as special. On summer days when it rained, farm work would cease early, and Dad would enter the house, saying, "Let's all go to Grandpa's!" We cleaned up a bit, piled in the car, and headed north about twenty-five miles. Grandma would greet us with open arms. "I thought you would come, since it rained!" Then she'd gather food from the cellar, and soon we'd have supper—nothing fancy, but lots of love. It had rained; we had gone to Grandpa's. On a rainy summer day, I still have this urge to "get up and go."

Pajama Ride

We have a once-in-a-while surprise for our children that we call the Pajama Ride. After the kids are in bed for about ten minutes, we go to their room and call out, "Pajama

Ride!" They get out of bed and we take them, in their pajamas, to a fun activity. One time we had prearranged to go to their grandparent's house for a treat. Another time we went to the Disneyland hotel, to look at the dancing water fountain. We have a rule that if the kids ask about it before bedtime, they won't have a Pajama Ride that night. It's a total-surprise treat.

Goof Day

When our son has a week or so of vacation from school, we set aside a special day and call it Goof Day. It means just what it says: We goof off. I let him plan where we go and where we will eat. It has turned out to be such a fun and exciting time for us, doing something together as Mom and son. We both look forward to it so much. The activity depends on the season, but we have gone to museums, ice-skated on the pond, and even worked together on a project he wanted to do at home. When his vacation begins, right away he says, "What day is our Goof Day, Mom?"

Celebrating a Rotten Day

Every so often, we celebrate a day that has been different. For instance, our son was in the first weeks of his freshman year of high school. We were fairly new to the community, and the previous year he had attended a Christian school. Bill didn't know very many people, and he was shy and uneasy.

Everything he did that morning seemed to go wrong; even his bicycle fell apart. We talked together about his doubts and fears and prayed together. He wanted to stay home and not go to school, but after some encouragement he consented to take my bicycle. His comment was, "I'll probably break that, too!"

Out the door he went with new resolve, only to return ten minutes later! Indeed, he *had* picked up a nail, and the tire was flat. By now there was not much time to get to school. I dropped what I was doing and took him, assuring him I'd be there to pick him up after school.

When I got home, I decided that such a day was worth celebrating. I planned his favorite food and baked his special bread, prepared the table in the dining room with decorations and a banner which read, BILL'S SPECIAL ROTTEN DAY. Everyone had a good time, and Bill was able to laugh at the problems. He still remembers this celebration and mentions how special it was.

Jolly Jaunts

When members of our family get into ruts or feel especially pressured with their responsibilities, I plan a Jolly Jaunt with them. A Jolly Jaunt is a special trip (from two hours to all-day long). Sometimes it is a total surprise to them, or sometimes I give just enough details to whet their appetite for "new hope." Some of our Jolly Jaunts have been:

- A picnic to a nearby lake, to feed the ducks.
- Lunch and shopping at quaint and unusual places.
- Going to small, out-of-the-way places for quiet and rest, giving time to share with no interruptions.

Somehow, after a Jolly Jaunt, things get into perspective again.

Wednesday-Morning Surprise

Every Tuesday night after my girls (ages nine and eleven) are asleep, I hide a small treat under their pillows. They look forward to waking up on Wednesday morning and finding this treat. It is always something inexpensive—a package of nuts, a stick of gum, a new pencil, or a small book.

A "Do" Box

When I was a child, there were often times when I would go to my mother and say, "What can I do now?" or, "There's nothing to do, Mom!" This would especially happen on rainy days or when I was recuperating from a childhood illness. Instead of reacting impatiently, Mom suggested that together we make a What Can I Do Now? box. We decorated a box with construction paper. Then we wrote, on separate papers, various activities that I could do—Straighten your room; read a book; draw a picture, and so forth. Whenever I was bored or restless, I could go to my box and draw out one of the pieces of paper. Usually the suggestion was sufficient to occupy me for a time.

Winter Picnic

To overcome the down time in January or February, we have a winter picnic. In the morning I make Jell-O salad, potato salad, and lettuce salad, stack them in the refrigerator and have hot dogs, buns, marshmallows, and sticks all ready. The checked tablecloth goes on the dining-room table and the picnic blanket on the living-room floor, in front of the fireplace. This is my surprise to the family, so they never know what day it might be. We cook the hot dogs and marshmallows and pop corn in the fireplace. We sing camp songs and reminisce about summer fun and have a great time. We have done this a number of years, and it works wonderfully! The only things we miss are the ants and the sand!

Rainy-Day Cookies

On rainy days when my children were young, we would always bake cookies. The older one would help me in the big oven. The twins had a little Easybake oven and made their own miniature cookies. When they were done, we'd all have a tea party.

6

Turning Work Into Fun

Whatever you do, do your work heartily, as for the Lord rather than for men.

Colossians 3:23 NAS

Come on; Let's Sing

Since I grew up in a family of seven, my job was often to do supper dishes—a mountain of them—alone. Being farmers, we ate late, and I hated that BIG job at that hour. My dad would often say, "Come on; I'll help you, and we'll sing." He knew I loved duetting with him. It really helped make the chore endurable. He had finished his chores and was no doubt tired, yet he was willing to meet my need.

Saturday-Night Accounting

Each Saturday night, my husband and his four sisters would gather around the table, and their father would get out a large sheet of yellow ledger paper. Each child would tell what kind of work he or she had done around the house or yard that week and approximately how many hours or minutes he or she had worked. Then their father would tally up how much money per hour or minute that particular job would be worth and write it on that child's page of earnings. The "money" went toward college.

Even the youngest girl, a preschooler at the time, had a page. Sometimes she could not think of anything she had done, and Mother would come to her rescue and say, "Well, Anna picked some flowers for me," or "Anna took her nap every day this week without fussing." My husband said it was a very important element in building not only the desire and appreciation for hard work, but more importantly, a healthy self-image for each child.

Missionary Pickles

During the time our six children were growing up together at home, we took on a family project of growing cucumbers, pickling them, and sending them to market. The proceeds were given to missionary friends whom our children also knew. This made working in the garden more like fun. We took pictures through the different stages of the project and made a poster of the children's participation. This, along with correspondence from our missionary friends on our children's level of understanding, added reward and fun to what could otherwise have been just another dreaded chore!

Together Day

My husband works many hours, so we can't do a lot of things together as a family. Thursday is my husband's payday, so that's the day we go marketing. That's also the only day we can be together, so I have made that day into our special Together Day. That morning we put on our best Levis. We go to the market, choosing our week's groceries together. Then we ride around town and finally go somewhere to eat. When we go home, we feel we have done something really special with one another. Our little boy really looks forward to our Together Day.

Spelling Bees in the Milk Truck

When I was just starting out in grade school, we had frequent spelling exams and many words to learn. My father drove a milk truck and had to pick up milk on Saturdays. We would all—Mom, Dad, my sister, and I—pile into the milk truck and go with him. As we sat high up in the big cab, Dad made the trip into a spelling contest. He would have us spell words until we were stumped. Then he would correct us and quiz us more. Consequently, spelling became fun and reading became easy, which was a big plus for my sister and me in high school and college.

Fall Apple Picking

Every fall, when the leaves begin to turn, my family's thoughts turn to apple cider and apple pies. Many years ago we decided that we would set aside one full Saturday to go apple picking. We study the maps together, to pick out a different orchard each year. When we arrive at the orchard, we stop to get our bucket first, and then off we go into the orchard. When our bucket is full, we know it's time to head home. Then the pies, apple sauce, and cider become a family project. This is something we all look forward to in the autumn.

Janet's Beets

During canning season, it's easier to get the four children to help with the canning if we read a book as a family. The oldest boy and I take turns reading out loud, while the rest continue cutting up the vegetables or fruit and putting them in the jars. Each child marks the jar he fills, and through the year we eat "Janet's beets" or "Charlie's beans." It helps turn a tedious task into an enjoyable time together, even though the youngest (who is six) comes up with odd shapes and sizes in his jars. The ones too little for a paring knife use a table knife and still do their bit according to their ability, and they think they've done as much as the older ones.

Work-With-Mother Day

As a mother of five girls, house chores had become a hassle for me. I found myself worn out from trying to be fair in instructing and supervising the girls to get their jobs done. A workable solution was reached when one summer I decided to spend one day with each of the three oldest girls. This is how it worked. Each of the girls chose a day to work with Mother. On her day, the daughter chose from a list of household chores that needed tending. If it was windows, she and Mother worked side by side till the job was complete. Or maybe it was drawers or the garage or the basement.

A special fellowship and communication took place between mother and daughter, and at the same time, I was able to individually instruct how each job should be done. The other daughters were assigned either to babysit the younger two or to do general tidying up and preparing lunch for the rest. By the end of the summer, the girls had become responsible about chores and our relationships had become special as we learned and worked together. It was surprising how many in-depth discussions we had as we worked. I started this when the three oldest were just seven, eight, and nine years old, and it has continued through their teen years.

Chores in a Sugar Bowl

Since I am a working mother, extra cleaning is left until Saturday. Not wanting to spend all day Saturday cleaning, we do what my mother did when I was a child. That is, chores are written on slips of paper and put in a sugar bowl. The chores may be: Wash dishes; vacuum; dust; clean bathroom. There are also slips of paper that say: Bake a cake; read a book for ten minutes; pick some flowers for the table; call Grandma. In this way, we all have fun, and still the house gets clean. As the girls have gotten older, they still like this method best for Saturday cleaning, instead of Mother assigning the different chores.

Yard Day

We lived in an apartment for eight years, but two years ago we moved into a house that has a big yard—half an acre. This was quite a shock, since we'd always had someone else do our yard work. But we decided to make lawn mowing and trimming day a special day. We work together as a family, and that evening, the children decide what they would like special for dinner, or we go out to eat at a place of their choice. This makes Yard Day a day for them to look forward to.

A Mug or a Bowl?

When asking my children to do something I knew they didn't want to do, I always tried to give them a choice on something concerning the job. For example: "Tim, do you want to use a red or blue towel with your bath?" "Sandy, do you want to drink your soup from a mug, or use a bowl?" The job got done, usually with no murmuring.

7

We Played Together

Let all who take refuge in you be glad; let them ever sing for joy. Spread your protection over them, that those who love your name may rejoice in you.

Psalms 5:11 NIV

Read to Us

As a child, I loved to read. My grandparents, who lived with us, were forever requesting that I read to them from the newspaper. I guess I felt adults were not the brightest people in the world! Then Grandfather would faithfully open the huge, heavy, family Bible and say, "Read this to us." He always found the passage to be read, but I was the one to read. This was my best memory of Grandfather and Grandmother. They instilled in me the love of Scripture. How wise they were! Today I am so grateful for that project the three of us shared together daily, on the steps of the old homestead.

Pasture Walk

Since our five children are young (sixteen months to nine years), we all still seem to enjoy walking through our fields and pasture or along a seldom-traveled dirt road. The smallest rides on Daddy's shoulders, thoroughly content. Others may take a bike or tricycle if they choose, but usually we all walk, not having a deadline to meet.

We notice anthills and mourning-dove nests. When creeks are dry, we climb through the tunnel under the bridge. One child especially likes to pick wild flowers. When wild plums, gooseberries, and mulberries are in season, we stop and eat. The three oldest children enjoy our pasture pond, and the little ones splash at the side.

Talking Fancy Pants

When I was a little girl, my dad started a beautiful project that has been expanded in our family. I hope it will become a tradition. He named my doll Fancy Pants. Then, sort of in *Winnie-the-Pooh* fashion, he created wonderful stories about my doll and her imaginary friends and family. Every night before I went to sleep, he would Talk Fancy Pants and then follow that time with a prayer time.

We now do this with our children, individually—but we have included all their bedtime friends that have received names from the children. The children also do some of the "talking" of their wonderful, imaginary friends, and we are hard pressed not to let an evening go by without this special time of sharing. The benefits: The children's interests, needs, and often their problems come forth so gently during this time. We then follow this time with their individual evening prayer time.

Twenty Summers

We have a family tradition that seems to have grown into a very important time for the children. About twenty years ago, when we were a very young family with three little girls ages one, two, and three, we discovered a beautiful spot on a lake in the mountains. We discovered it to be a perfect and inexpensive place for a family to be together with nature. It wasn't easy, camping with babies, carrying in all the baby paraphernalia—high chairs, playpens, and diaper pails. Every night there were dirty babies to bathe. Afterward, Daddy gave the clean child a piggyback ride to the tent. Even when they were so big their feet would touch the ground, they expected this.

As our family grew to ten children, we kept going there every year. They have wonderful memories of learning to row a boat, catching their first fish, watching a lightning storm on the lake, and so forth. Most of all, they still look forward to at least one time each year when they can all be together. Even now, as some of them have grown up and married, they bring their husbands and families along, too.

My husband and I feel that it was worth the personal inconveniences and irritations, to have those times of closeness. We haven't missed a summer in twenty years.

Summer Breakfast in the Park

One thing that I'm sure my children will always remember is early summer mornings in the neighborhood park, eating breakfast and playing together. Little ones like to wake up with the sun; Mom likes to sleep. So one morning a week in the summer, I packed breakfast, and off we went. It was so peaceful, early in the morning in the park. I had my devotions quietly, while the three children were swinging and enjoying one another.

Restaurant Game

When taking our six children on a trip, we have a game we play in restaurants. Each in turn orders his meal and hands the menu to the waitress, remembering the price of one another's orders, so they can guess what the total bill will be. The one guessing closest wins a prize of a dollar. In the meantime, all six are quiet, orderly, and beginning to realize what it takes for a family of eight to eat out. Our five-year-old gloats because, being last to guess, even he guesses it by accident, once in a while.

Create a Memory

My husband and I embarked on a project to "create a memory" with our fifteen-year-old son and thirteen-year-old daughter. Each one of us had a separate memory we planned to create, but we all participated in one another's memory. We planned it by writing an outline, delegating plans and work involved in the memory, and contributing to the excitement and anticipation of the forthcoming event.

Example: Our thirteen-year-old wanted a weekend pack trip to a mountain lake. We delegated the car and pack items to Dad and the fishing gear to son. I handled the menu and food. The thirteen-year-old and I handled the clothes packing and sleeping gear. We picked a date several weeks in advance. During this time there were the usual conflicts between brother and sister, but any quarreling relating to the memory was off limits. We became aware that any word or action could totally ruin someone's permanent memory. The project was a total success. We became more aware of one another's feelings and desires and of the ability we had for building memories into one another's lives.

Father's Stories

When I was growing up, my father would make up stories for my brother and me. We would each give him three words—sometimes related, sometimes not, sometimes serious, sometimes silly. Sometimes the stories he made up had a moral to them; other times they were merely entertaining. I hold fond memories of these story times designated just for us, since my father was a very busy man.

Mother Joined our Play

When I was a child, my mother joined in our play at times when many mothers would have become angry, instead. For example, my little brother and I had been blowing bubbles in the kitchen. Eventually this made the floor slippery. We then began sliding around on the floor. When Mom came to the door, she stood quietly at the door for a few seconds, sizing up the situation, then took off her shoes, took a running start, laughed, and slid past us all! I've loved her for it ever since. Her childlikeness is and was special. (P.S. After the play was over, we got to clean up the floor!)

Dad's Classics

After supper, my dad would tell my brother and me a story—one of the great literary classics, which he simplified into words we could understand. It was a continuous story, and each evening he would pick up the tale and review in two or three sentences the previous evening's portion and then continue with another portion. Summer evenings we sat out on a side porch and devoured every word he related. We could ask questions or try to guess what was going to happen. It was not until many years later that I learned what great books these simple stories were. Some were even Greek myths.

In addition to the closeness I felt with my brother and dad, the main value was that I was able to do the same in a small way with my two small daughters, many years later. Although I was not the accomplished storyteller my dad was, I embellished, as well as I could, any stories I told my girls. This seemed to help them develop a love of books, and they have both been avid readers of fine books. The older one, now in university, is studying Shakespeare and loves it. The younger, a senior in high school, is also heavily into literature, and most of their spending money is used in bookstores.

8

Memories of Togetherness

Blessed be the Lord, who daily loadeth us with benefits, even the God of our salvation.

Psalms 68:19

Turning Inconvenience Into Fun

On the farm when I was a child, there were a number of times during winter months when the electricity would go off because of weather conditions. At this point, if it were evening, Mom would get out some candles and Dad, Mom, and we three kids would play table games. I still remember the fun we had. Rather than being afraid or upset when the power went off, we would be excited! It taught me the value of playing as a family—even if our electricity doesn't go off.

Cool-Off Break

One of my best memories of time together as a family when I was growing up was hot summer days. After we had been playing outside and needed a Cool-Off Break, my mother would gather us together on the cool kitchen floor. She would read continuing stories—*The Wind in the Willows* or *The Yearling,* and so forth. This created a peaceful, unified specialness, which we all shared as we cooled off together.

Adjusting Pains

When we moved to a new school, we three children were having "adjusting pains." Mother put a large double bed in our family room. Every night, all five of us would sit on this bed together. Two of us would sit on Mom's and Dad's laps, and the third child would sit between Mom and Dad. We would all hold hands.

As we read and talked together, one of us would squeeze another's hand, and he would pass it on to another, until everyone had received the unspoken message of love and acceptance. All the problems we had at school were bearable because of the warmth and acceptance we received each night in our home. We continued with this long after the original need had been met and even loved doing this at times in our teens.

Together, Alone

My husband pastors a small church, and our family is grown. His study is in our house, and the house is next door to the church. Unofficially, I'm his assistant in many areas. We have a lot of being together in our work, which sometimes leads to a deteriorating personal togetherness. Because we work together so many hours, we almost have a sense of guilt about planning time for personal togetherness.

One of our most precious times has been developed this

fall. Early in the morning, he builds a fire in the fireplace in the lower-floor recreation room, and we spend our quiet time together—each separate, but together. The friendliness of that setting at five in the morning warms more than our toes. The physical proximity we experience as we work together is not always "togetherness." We find that to plan special times together is an even greater need as we get older and ever busier than in our younger years.

Opening Mail Together

My husband is a man of many interests, so when he gets home from work, he is busy with chores and the garden or other hobbies. We have discovered one secret to making sure we sit still together every evening after dinner. We have promised each other that we will open our daily mail together. Previously, I used to pick it up at the post office, rip open my personal letters, and throw away the junk mail, so it seemed Ronnie missed out altogether on the treat of opening our mail. Now we find that the time together leads into all sorts of discussions, which otherwise would never occur.

Family Conferences

The main activity in our family that has fostered deeper communication and fellowship has been our family conferences. Any individual in the family can call a conference, at any time he feels a need for one. Everyone has come to feel free to share his deep, heartfelt needs during these times. A conference may be only a few minutes, or it may be hours of digging, to get to the root of problems. Once the air is cleared and, if necessary, forgiveness has been asked, this has set the climate for some of our most enjoyable times of fellowship, fun, and oneness. If one member can't sleep because of a problem for which he needs help, he can feel free to get the family up for a conference.

Dinner With Daddy at Work

My husband works long and late hours, so our family doesn't get to be together in the evening at all. Our three daughters asked if we could surprise Daddy at his five o'clock lunch and bring him a dinner. After getting the meal ready, we packed the dishes, napkins, and food, and off we went to surprise Daddy. He not only liked our surprise, but asked if we would eat dinner with him again. For the last two years, we have eaten dinner with Daddy at least four out of seven times a week: happy Daddy, happy kids, and happy me!

I Like You Because. . . .

My husband and I wanted to help encourage a sense of unity and appreciation among our children. The children get along fairly well, but they are all such achievers that we felt they needed to feel they each had a special place with the others, regardless of achievements or competitive factors. We began by suggesting that each child voluntarily express what he or she liked or appreciated about each one of the others. We got more than we had bargained for! They were most expressive. We could sense the love and relaxing security it brought to each child. Even the ones who feel things deeply said quite a bit, and it opened up an avenue for expression of our deep love and appreciation for one another.

We do this on special holidays and occasionally in between—just enough to keep it very special. However, as an outgrowth, we have noticed that the children write thank-you and appreciation notes to each other now and also openly write words of appreciation on their memo boards in their rooms. The attitude has caught on!

Replacing Undesirable Activity

During our daughters' school days, we developed a great sense of togetherness as a family. When unacceptable activities were planned at school, my husband and I arranged our schedule to go on an outing—a picnic or a similar activity— to give our time and attention to our daughters. Replacing an undesirable situation with an enjoyable family-fun time helped them not feel isolated or left out. In their adulthood, they still recall these times and express their appreciation for them, knowing their parents really cared. This was one thing that helped to build a good relationship among family members and has aided communications and confidence.

Giggles and Squeals

We have a Family-Together Time each evening, which lasts thirty to forty-five minutes. About one hour before the children's bedtime, I get them in their pjs. Then we have hugging, tumbling, and loving on the living room floor. Our children love physical contact, so this is really a fun time, with lots of giggles and squeals. Then we wind down with songs about love and Jesus, read a story, have a treat, and clean up for "night-night." Then we go down to each child's room and have prayers.

This whole program seems to have eliminated any bedtime fussiness, because they have our time and reassurances that they are special. They all fall asleep much sooner and very seldom wake up during the night. It has helped my husband and me to feel fulfilled as parents and to see how important it is to our little ones to be shown love through spending this time together, instead of watching TV.

Nickel Night

When our children were small, we had so many hassles getting them to bed, especially on warm evenings. We dreamed up Nickel Night. The child in bed first that evening, with his teeth brushed, his clothes in the hamper, and all, got a nickel. The one who got twenty-five cents first had the privilege of going to the soda shop with Mom or Dad for a special treat. This stopped the poking and hassles, and since the children never knew when Nickel Night would be announced, it helped them be prompt each night in getting ready for bed. Going to bed became a fun game. We did this for years. It made for family togetherness, Mom was not uptight, the kids were happy, bedtime prayers were said in a happy frame of mind. Bedtime became special.

How Was School?

When my husband and I asked our school-age children, "How did school go?" they would always answer, "Just fine." So we instigated a game to encourage more family sharing. At the dinner table, each child is given a precise time of day, such as 10:45 A.M., and he then fills in with what he was doing at just that time. It has turned out to be a fun time of telling, not only for the children, but for the parents, too. The children also gave my husband and me a certain time, and we were to tell what we had been doing at that time.

Doughnut Day

At our house, the first snowy day of winter became the day to make a big batch of doughnuts. The children always loved it. It all started with my own mother making doughnuts for us when school would be closed because of snow. It was a nice time for us, as a family, and it was always fun to share the doughnuts with friends. This tradition is such fun for all of us.

PART 3

HOW MY PARENTS MADE GOD AN IMPORTANT PART OF OUR HOME

9

Family Time With God

And you shall love the Lord your God with all your heart and with all your soul and with all your might. And these words, which I am commanding you today, shall be on your heart; and you shall teach them diligently to your sons and shall talk of them when you sit in your house and when you walk by the way and when you lie down and when you rise up.

Deuteronomy 6:5–7 NAS

"Mom! Dad! Time to Get Up!"

As a typical Christian family, we were having trouble maintaining a consistent family devotional time. It seemed that the mornings were so hectic. My husband and I knew that, since the boys were getting older (twelve and nine), it was imperative we make this an important part of our family life and, together, put the Lord first.

We had a family council and decided that 7:00 each morning was to be the time, the living room, the place. The first person there was to have the responsibility of calling the others. This included permission for our boys to chide us parents, if need be, with, "It's time for our Bible study. Remember, the Lord and the rest of the family are more important than sleep."

The boys love getting us up, and our devotional time has

flourished because of it. It has given us a real commitment to one another. We want our boys to recall that putting God first is a rewarding thing.

Around the Kitchen Table

When it rained or it was too cold for outside activities on Sunday afternoons, our entire family of nine would gather around the kitchen table. Dad opened a large, family picture Bible and put his hand over the words, so we could see only the picture. The youngest child had the first chance to tell what the picture was about. If he didn't know, the next youngest one was allowed to tell the story. This created a special interest for Bible stories, we learned a lot—from the littlest on up—and we had a wonderful time together.

Family Time With God

We designed a Family Time With God calendar, to help us develop a more consistent devotional life as a family. Using a poster board, I made little pockets (seven in each of five rows) out of construction paper. Into these we placed a piece of paper with the Scripture verse or activity for that night. Each month the children help me decorate the calendar. Each slip of paper put in the pockets sticks up over the pocket, and we decorate that part according to the holidays or special events for the month. Then the children get to take turns pulling out the slips of paper to be read each night. It has given us structure for our devotional time and helped us to be more consistent.

Attitude for the Day

My parents believed the attitude a person has for each day has most likely been set the night before. So, as a family, we set aside a special time together each evening—sometimes sharing, sometimes reading, sometimes singing—but always making sure we had cleared any offenses toward one another that may have accumulated that day. Then Dad would ask for personal prayer requests and someone prayed the requests. Usually we took turns.

To add to this attitude for the day, in the morning, Mother played Christian music on the stereo and then came cheerfully to our rooms, to announce that it was time to get up. This music really added to the atmosphere of our home in the morning. When the stereo was broken and there was no music in the morning, we really missed it.

These were two simple things that made our home a peace-filled place that was a calm haven for us all to come home to.

Our Song and the Prayer Board

We have been blessed with seven children. There have been times when we did not value one another as we should. To encourage a knowledge of one another's worth, we sing what the children call Our Song.

We sing it nine times, all looking directly into the eyes of one member each time. This has done a great deal to bring us closer together. Often there are tears in our eyes, as we sing with appreciation for the other person.

From this, we developed our Prayer Board. It has a cup
hook under each of our names. On the hook goes the name
of the person we are responsible to pray for that week. At
the end of the week, we redraw names.

These two things have really drawn our nine together as a
loving, caring family.

Our Family-Proverbs Project

Every day we read one chapter of Proverbs out loud in
our family-circle time and then ask questions about the
chapter. For every right answer, a penny is put into our missionary bank, to add to our regular gift to a special family
missionary. The children are now old enough to read out
loud, so they take their turns reading and asking questions.
Oh, how they love to test Mom and Dad. They get great joy
in counting the money at the end of each week. This has become a very special project in our family. It has helped our
family in so many areas, such as:

- Reading and listening ability
- Discerning wisdom and foolishness
- Bringing a closeness to our family that we would
  otherwise have missed
- Giving time for the children to ask questions about
  Scripture and share problems they are having.
  They often hear a Proverb that deals with a simi-
  lar problem.
- Encouraging more openness with one another

Putting on Armor

Every morning, before we get up, my husband and I re-peat the Twenty-third Psalm and put on the whole armor of God by reciting Ephesians 6:11–18. This has given us real strength for the day and a oneness with the Lord and each other.

Family Devotions: A Joy

We want our family devotions to be a time our children will remember with joy, so we vary our methods. Right now, each child and parent is responsible for devotions one night of the week. I provide a Bible storybook, a Bible, some simpler Bible storybooks for young readers, quiz cards, Bible-verse cards, and cards with the books of the Bible on them. When it is his turn for devotions, a child may choose a story to be read by him or a parent, decide on another activ-ity, and lead the prayer time. They really enjoy leading, on their night.

We parents also use other methods, such as pictures or a flannelgraph, which makes for variety. If the children get hung up on one activity, we try to get them to work on other things, such as learning the books of the Bible or studying quiz cards.

Prayer by the Day

Realizing we were not sharing or caring for one another's needs, we made a card for each person in the family, with his name in bold letters. Then we designated one day a week for each person. On his day, we put his name card on the refrigerator door, indicating it was his special day for our prayers. Since Dad taught Sunday school, his name was on the door on Sundays. We all prayed for Dad on Sunday. Mike had a discipling Bible study during lunch hour on Thursday, so that was his day. Rod had a spelling test every Friday and wanted that day. With six people in the family, we each had a day, leaving one day to pray for Grandma and Grandpa, who lived next door.

We learned to share our needs with one another and pray for one another. The name on the refrigerator didn't mean dishes or garbage detail; it meant, "You're special—we're all praying for you today!"

Morning Blessing

My husband prays individually for each of our two boys and me before he leaves for work. Usually we are seated at the table for breakfast. He comes around to each, lays his hand on our shoulder, and prays a short prayer specifically remembering that person's activities that day. It really is a neat way for us to begin the day, and the Lord is bringing our family closer to one another through this.

Turning Thoughts to God

In our home, we use a small bulletin board to put up Bible verses or related thoughts. It is placed on the wall near a frequently used doorway. I print up quotes from outstanding men of God from other eras or today, or meaningful

Bible verses, changing it two or three times a week. I make sure they are attractive and eye-catching and large enough to see across the room.

The family contributes ideas, which I love to use. If we are going through a special trial, we gear our helps to that. The one up this week is: Lord, use the hurts and pressures of today to crowd me close to Yourself.

My husband and two teenage children make frequent comments of the help this is to them in turning their thoughts toward the Lord.

Psalm-Singing Family

A real highlight for our family has been putting Scripture to melody. It started when a young-people's Bible study that we have in our home was studying the Psalms. Our oldest son reminded my husband, who teaches this study, that he knew a Psalm that was put to melody. This was the beginning. My husband, who plays the guitar, put Psalm one to music for the first Bible study. It was so delightful that we taught it to the whole church. Since that time, our oldest son has put a Psalm to melody, and several others in the Bible-study group added their creations.

Our family sings these Psalm songs on car trips together, and we have made up a song sheet that we use for our Bible-study group, though we have long since finished our study of the Psalms. We have become the Psalm-Singing Family! We expect that, for our children, this will be one happy memory of God in their childhood.

10

The Power of Example

In everything set them an example by doing what is good. In your teaching show integrity, seriousness and soundness of speech that cannot be condemned, so that those who oppose you may be ashamed because they have nothing bad to say about us.

Titus 2:7, 8 NIV

Always There to Love

When I was a child and did something for which I needed to be spanked, my mother spanked me, then had me sit alone quietly for five or ten minutes, thinking about what I had done and the punishment I had received for having done it. Then, after a few minutes, Mother would come over to me, hug me, tell me she loved me and that she was sorry she had to spank me. Through this, I learned that with wrongdoing came correction, but not condemnation, for my mother was always there to love and forgive me. What an example she was to me of the gentle but firm love and consistency of my heavenly Father.

Hurt in His Eyes

My father was a wise man, who taught me a lifelong and helpful lesson. When I would misbehave, eventually it would be time to face Dad—which I really dreaded. Dad would look at me with such hurt in his eyes. Then he would express how much he loved me and how sad I made him when I did wrong. He rarely disciplined in any other way, but his talks and his looks hurt me more than many spankings would have and made me stop and think of what I had done.

As I grew into my teen years, I would think of my father's loving hurt each time I was tempted to do wrong, and the thought of hurting him kept me from many wrong choices. Now, in my adult years, I like to relate this to the hurt I cause my heavenly Father when I do wrong. What a strength in temptation this thought is.

First Corinthians 13

When dating my husband, I designed a chart incorporating the qualities of love mentioned in 1 Corinthians 13, to enable me to better meet his needs. For example, "Love is patient. . . ." was followed by a list of ways in which I could show patience to him. "Love is kind. . . ." was followed by specific acts of kindness I could do for him. I tried to be very specific as to his personal needs. As I grew to know him better, I was able to add other helps in each category. Through the years of our marriage, I have added more to the list and have begun lists for other close relationships—sister, parents, friends.

Early-Morning Quiet Time

My husband and I get up an hour early each morning to have Bible study and prayer together. Our three-year-old daughter is an early riser and usually comes out before we're finished. We save her some hot chocolate. She gives us a big smile and sits quietly with her books until we're finished. She is getting the idea that Bible study is important. If we're finished when she gets up, she asks disappointedly, "Did you already have Bible study?" We want her to remember this early morning Bible study as a happy, satisfying time, so that someday it will be a satisfying part of her daily routine, too.

Never a Harsh Word

I have good memories of my father, who has never spoken a harsh word to my mother. I can never remember that he spoke harsh or unkind words about others, either. He was the head of our home—strong, generous, and kind. He has been a great influence in my life. God was an important part of our home, not only because we talked about Him, but my father showed us what He was like. Because of my father's example, I've also been able to control my anger and a sharp tongue.

The Security of Jesus' Name

When our daughter was one year old, we began to share a Bible time with her each night before bedtime. She loves her Bible and is so excited each night. She runs and points to it and can hardly wait for her story. Four months later, she now says "Bible" and "Jesus"—smiling, as if His name brings warmth and security and love. Before this, bedtime was a trying time, with much crying. Now, after her Bible time, she snuggles up, says good night, and closes her eyes for the night. It's a joy to see how this time we share together is bringing such peace and contentment, in contrast to the fear and rebellion of before. Also, I know we are helping her develop a love of and a desire for God's Word and the concept that Jesus loves her, plus helping to set a pattern for developing a consistent time for her daily devotions.

Evening Prayer

About two years ago, we started an evening prayer time for our family. This has become a warm and meaningful experience. It has drawn us together as a family. Our children have learned to take everyday things to God in prayer and to look for definite answers.

Here is how it works. The children are ready for bed and in their beds, and we sit on their beds. Usually one of the girls (ages four and eight) starts the prayer, then the other girl, then myself, then my husband. Our little boy is twenty months old. He cuddles down with us and enjoys the security of this warm time together.

Some evenings, if it gets a little late, we will say, "Let's have one person pray for us all," but we never skip this prayer time. When we have company staying over, including them in our prayer time is our special way of welcoming them into our home.

PART 4

HOW WE MADE
EACH OTHER
FEEL SPECIAL

11

Our Kitchen Was a
Special Place for Love

Behold, how good and how pleasant it is for brethren to dwell together in unity!

Psalms 133:1

One Small Pie Tin

The two main expressions of love that I remember from my childhood are related to food. They were personal acts my mother and grandmother did for me repeatedly. As a very small child, I remember sitting in the kitchen every morning and watching my mother squeeze orange juice for me. As I look back on this, it is very precious.

My grandmother had one small pie tin. Whenever she made pie, she always made a miniature pie in the small tin, just for me. What made these acts so memorable is that they were just for me, they were something I could watch as they were prepared, and the same thing was done repeatedly, over a number of years.

My Best Thing

I grew up in a family with two brothers, seven and eight years older than I. My folks always made our dinner times fun and special. I remember that when I was little, I would sometimes be left out of the conversation, because I was so much younger. But this didn't happen very often, because my mother initiated the idea of each of us sharing My Best Thing. We would each take a turn and tell the best thing that happened to us that day. Sometimes I could hardly wait for the family to be together, so I could share My Best Thing.

More Than an Orange

My mother always took time to make simple things extra special. I have happy memories of asking for an orange and then delighting to see she had cut it into a lovely basket shape and filled it with the fruit. This made me feel special and loved.

Treats for the Whole Team

During our son's school years, he delighted in bringing friends home often and was especially happy when treats were available. Most of the time I was glad he was so hospitable, but sometimes it was difficult to have snacks available every day for the whole "team." He and I worked out a plan. Wednesdays, after school, he could be sure that special treats would be prepared for him and as many friends as he wanted to bring home. Sometimes I decorated the table and made name cards with Scripture verses for each place. It was a great encouragement to our son and a means to witness to his friends, who also became my friends. His friends were always welcome, but Wednesdays, they could count as special.

Snooping in the Pots

My kitchen is a special place for love. When my big, teenage boys come snooping before dinner, looking in the pots and saying, "What's cooking, Mom?" I make it an occasion to give them a big hug or a warm kiss. Even if my hands are full of flour or I have many "irons in the fire," I drop what I'm doing and wash my hands. One son has come to expect this attention and often will even ask for a hug while I fix supper.

We have found that teenagers need to be hugged and kissed regularly, even though they may not initiate it (not in front of friends, of course).

First Day of School

Rather than making the first day of school a time to dread, I decorated the kitchen with crepe paper, made a special breakfast, and left each child new pencils at his place setting. When they left for school, we all formed a circle at the door and prayed together. If their friends had come to walk to school with them, they were included in our prayer circle.

A Warm Pie Tin

After I graduated from high school, both my dad and I worked late hours. The family couldn't wait dinner for us, so there was always a warm pie tin—covered with foil and filled with a tasty dinner—in the oven, waiting for us when we got home. Then Mom would come to the table and listen to the happenings of our day, as we enjoyed eating a hot meal.

Pie Day

For many years, I baked pies every Thursday. We often had more pies than we needed. I planned it that way. Every Thursday would be Pie Day, and the children and I would deliver a pie to a friend or neighbor. Since we were new in the neighborhood, it was an excellent way to get to know our neighbors. It was a great way to teach the children the art of introducing themselves to new friends, the blessing of sharing material things the Lord had given us, and the importance of reaching out to others with God's love. From sharing on Pie Day, we were blessed with one friendship that eventually led to another person receiving Christ as her personal Savior. How we all rejoiced, that one of our pies helped bring someone to Christ.

More Filling Than Bread

Each day, when I packed lunches for my family, I made it a point to pack a good sandwich—one with more filling than bread—and all the rest that goes with a good lunch. This is something that I did all through our children's school years, and frankly, I never knew it was meaningful, until my twenty-year-old daughter told me so recently. She said her lunch was always the envy of her schoolmates, especially of her best friend, who always had peanut butter and jelly.

Candy Day

Years ago we instituted Candy Day, to eliminate the problem of everyone eating candy too frequently. Friday became Candy Day! After our dinner, if we happened to have a box of candy, each member of our family selected a piece from the candy box. Each one could hardly wait to find out if there were new selections or what someone else would choose. We had a good time, eating our special treat together, and had a special sense of togetherness. We all looked forward to family decision time—nuts? cream? bar?

Occasionally we would give each child fifteen cents (those were the days of nickel candy bars). They could then buy their own treat that week. We specified that one item must be fruit or nuts. This occasional surprise eliminated begging for candy every time we shopped.

Candy Day worked beautifully for years. The older children gave up candy voluntarily, as they became more conscious of waistlines and nutrition in high school, but during the early years, Candy Day really limited their sweet intake, and our shopping trips were much more pleasurable.

One day a neighbor gave our daughter a candy bar, and she wouldn't eat it. She told them excitedly, "Oh, this will be saved for Candy Day!"

Saturday-Night Goodie

As children, we always looked forward to sitting around the dining-room table on Saturday evening to enjoy some goodie my parents bought out of their meager income. It was our only treat for the week. We anticipated this special time with eager expectation. I remember my father telling us that his family did the same thing; each week, they shared a bag of coconut drops.

12

T-I-M-E Spells Love

God is not unjust; he will not forget your work and the love you have shown him as you have helped his people and continue to help them.

Hebrews 6:10 NIV

Spoil Day

Because I had seven brothers and sisters, everything that came to our house had to be shared: treats and gifts, even love and attention. It seemed I could never gain the full, complete, and undivided attention of my mother without another one of my sisters or brothers coming along and stealing some of *my* time.

So the Lord gave my mother the creative idea to incorporate a new annual holiday—Spoil Day. This isn't as bad as it sounds (actually, we kids gave it this name). Once a year, either my mother or my father would take just one of us out for the whole day and allow us to plan the day's events. This way we had our parent's full, undivided attention for practically twenty-four hours!

On one of my Spoil Days, I chose to go shopping with my mom in a quaint town. I got to choose where I wanted to eat, and I usually wrapped up the day munching on a special treat that had been purchased just for *me*. I brought a small

gift back home with me that was just for *me,* to remember
my special Spoil Day.

Early Risers

My self-employed husband works six days a week. As our
family has increased, he has had great difficulty finding a
way to spend that much needed, one-to-one time alone with
each child. We had discussed this, but hadn't come up with
an answer. During the summer months, my husband discovered that he enjoyed early rising, as it gave him the opportunity to work on projects around the house. It also sparked an
idea for solving his time-alone problem with the children.
Now, completely unplanned, he will rise early one morning
and awaken one child. They silently slip out of the house
and go out to breakfast. The child that goes also gets the
added benefit of choosing a small treat for the other three at
home. The ones at home love hearing all the restaurant details from the chosen child, and Dad and child have a wonderful time alone.

Contented Sick Children

Throughout the school year, whenever one of the children
is sick, I take it as an opportunity to minister to that child
individually and specially. We have seven children, so this
time is valuable to both the child and me. The quiet time together usually leads to their sharing of spiritual needs, de-
feats, questions, problems, and fears. Each time, I have
found that this quiet time for communication was needed. It
would turn up hidden problems I had been aware of, but

had not gotten through, until this time. Being away from his brothers and sisters gave the child freedom to share. I have very contented sick children! Now I get excited whenever one is sick, for I know God is in control and is using this sickness for a good purpose.

I suppose some children might take advantage of this time and want to stay home, yet so far, our children have not taken advantage of this special time.

An Only Child

Since I was an only child, my mother understood that going to bed was sometimes a lonely time for me, especially when I heard the talking and giggles that came from my parents' bedroom.

She used to come into my room on Friday nights, when I didn't have to be up early for school the next day. We would talk and sing together, laugh and tell jokes. Sometimes she would gently rub my back. I would share things with her that I didn't at any other time. I never minded being alone in my bedroom the rest of the week, when I had Friday night to look forward to.

Mom's Time

I start each day by asking my family, "Who has a need of my time as Mother today?" or, "What can I do for you today?" I'm surprised to find that the really small things are the most important. They want a special food for dinner or a certain story read that night, or maybe a pair of pants sewed for them to wear the next day. With my husband, it's usually a request that I take time to sit down and listen to him alone or maybe watch a ball game with him—just some time he doesn't have to share with the boys. He works six days a week, and I do, too; we have discovered this is a good way of making sure each person has some of Mom's time.

He Shared Every Minute

Since our son started school, I had been disappointed that he was not eager to share his day's activities. I had always had a very close relationship with my mother and would be very anxious to run home and tell her my happy and sad moments. I wanted this same sharing relationship with my son and daughter.

One evening we decided to turn off the TV, get out our big sleeping bags, and have a slumber party. With lights out, we took turns sharing the events of our day with one another. I shared; my daughter shared. When it was my son's turn, he went on and on: "Then the teacher said . . . . Then I said . . . . Then she said." He very thoroughly shared every minute of the day! As we talked later, he said, "That was so much fun. When can we do it again?" We have repeated this several times. Besides being a unique fun time together, it has encouraged him to share more and more with me when he gets home from school. This makes for a happier mother *and* child.

No Mothering

Before our eldest daughter was married, I took her on a short trip—just the two of us. Driving leisurely down the

Oregon coast, we stopped wherever and whenever one of us felt like it. We collected shells and driftwood, walked in the sand, and waded in the ocean; we even wound up swimming in our clothes. I made a vow that I would not mother her on the trip. I tried very hard not to criticize her, as I had done all her growing-up years. We talked at times, thought a lot, and really got to know each other as adults. It was a healing time for us also, because we needed to forgive each other for many things we had done and said that hurt each other. One by one, these things surfaced as we talked. We both look back on this as one of the best times of our lives. I would like to do this with our other children, as time and circumstances will allow. I need this time, and so do they!

Mother Was Ours

My mother used to devote the day before school started to my sister and me. Whatever we wanted to do, mother would do with us. Sometimes we went downtown and had an ice-cream cone, sometimes we played in the sandbox. It didn't matter what we did; all we cared was that Mother was *ours* for the whole day.

Saturdays Alone

My husband and I have made it a practice for years to rotate Saturdays alone with each of our four children. We go shopping or do a fun thing of their choosing for the day. The plan was to have individual time alone with each child, to listen to him, and to do what he was interested in doing. Now, as our children are getting older, they come to us with their money saved up, wanting to take *us* out for the day because it has meant so much to them.

No Lectures on a Date

As a child and through my teens and college years, my father did something I will never forget. Since he traveled a great deal and had six children, he felt a special need to find a way to stay close to us and to understand us. He did it by asking each of us, individually, to go on a date with him alone. We could sometimes pick what we'd like to do, or he would have something already planned. While together, he would ask questions such as, "What is on your mind these days?" He always communicated interest and love. We could freely share joys or problems and expect understanding and help, but no lecture. You don't lecture on a date!

Some of my richest memories are these dates with Daddy. My husband and I now do this with our two little ones, taking them one at a time to do something special. Our children are now five and seven, and they love it.

Taking them on errands doesn't count, unless the focus is on being with them!

Shopping: A Disaster

We have three sons, ages eleven, thirteen, and fifteen. Taking them shopping for school clothes was always a disaster. Each was interested in his own thing and bored and restless with the others'. A couple of years ago, I decided to take each separately. On that day, he could choose a special place for lunch—wherever he wanted to go. We rarely eat out, even at fast-food restaurants, so this is really a treat for us. The boys are learning how to act in a nice restaurant. Even if the shopping trip isn't totally successful, we have an enjoyable day. I am able to give each son individual attention in a relaxed, grown-up atmosphere, and he feels really special, too.

13

The Joys of Belonging to an Extended Family

May the God who gives endurance and encouragement give you a spirit of unity among yourselves as you follow Christ Jesus, so that with one heart and mouth you may glorify the God and Father of our Lord Jesus Christ.

Romans 15:5, 6 NIV

Gifts for Grandchildren

At the beginning of the year, each of our six grandchildren can request something he or she wants my husband or me to make for him during the year—such as a quilt, a giant-sized cushion, a chair, a desk. This then becomes that year's Christmas present.

This gives them the joy of choosing and also keeps them from asking for things too often. No one is jealous of what the other receives, since it has been his own choice to receive something else. It also gives my husband and me something to work on and plan during the year. We do it joyfully, with love, knowing it is something that will please that grandchild.

Little Sis

There were nine years between my younger sister and me. The age gap made her feel left out of a lot of things my older sister and I enjoyed, with our two-year age difference. Sensing her loneliness, I would ask her to go for an Adventure Walk (we lived in the country). I would summon her secretly, by a nickname that signaled the purpose of the walk was for sharing—not just a hurried trip to the mailbox or the neighborhood store.

We agreed on the nicknames Kiddo for her and Butch for me. When she sensed a need to share in private, she would use my nickname, and we would go for an Adventure Walk. First we would notice several things in nature that had changed since our last walk, and eventually the problem would come up. We found we shared better by taking this approach.

Another sister was born nine years later. Since I had left home by then, she became Butch. A special bond is still felt when one of us is addressed by this "signal" nickname. It's still the signal to find a quiet place to talk or to go for an Adventure Walk.

Love Sitting

In three years of marriage, my daughter-in-law has had three children. Though she is an excellent and loving mother, she has mentioned that it's easier to stay home than take the children anywhere alone.

So that I could get better acquainted with my grandchildren and also share love with my daughter-in-law, I have

begun Love Sitting with my grandchildren one day a week,
all day. The children and I have a delightful time enjoying
one another, and it gives their mother a chance to be an
adult for a few hours. I also prepare dinner for them, if she is
gone till late in the afternoon.

I'm growing in love and appreciation for my daughter-in-
law's many abilities and loving attitudes.

Thank You, Mom

Last year I sent a dozen red carnations to my husband's
mother on *my husband's birthday,* with a note: "Thank you,
Mom, for Charlie!"

She is still talking about it to everyone.

P.S. We used to have mother-in-law problems. They are
no more!

Enough Love

One of my daughters-in-law is an only child. When she
married into our family of five boys, she had a very hard
time believing that I had enough love to add her "in." She
kept trying to wring a promise from me that I would never
love anyone more than I did her. Well, another son got
married and the youngest went into the service, and I was
giving extra attention to these two, when I got a letter from
her. All her hurts and fears and, yes, even a little hateful-
ness, was dumped into my lap.

My first reaction was to lash back, but thank God, I
thought about it before I acted. What the Holy Spirit led me
to do was to write a corny poem, telling her that I had five

beloved children—all with special needs. I could run myself ragged, trying to meet each little desire and need, or I could be myself and just love each one with all my heart and know they would understand and love me back the way I was. It worked.

That was four years ago, and we have a super relationship. How very thankful I am that I didn't react in the wrong way. She often reminds me of the incident and has my poem in her scrapbook. She's a mother herself, now, and how pleased I am to see the gentleness she shows with her baby.

A Grandmother's Intercession

I am a grandmother whose children and grandchildren live in another state. Last Christmas I made my annual visit to be with my daughter, son-in-law, and three grandchildren. On the day I was to leave them again, I spent a great deal of time thinking of each one of them and their potentials—both for man and God. So, at the evening meal, I asked if I might lead the family devotions after dinner. Permission was gladly given.

I don't believe we have ever had a more meaningful time together, spiritually. It was a time of praise, thanksgiving, and intercession for each one individually, as I enumerated for each one his God-given talents and possibilities, as I saw them. Then I interceded for each one individually. The oneness we felt (between tears) was of the Lord, and we were brought closer together than ever before in that sweet communion. Family ties were strengthened and love flowed! God's Spirit made it all possible.

Little Brother

After I graduated from college and moved out to live with a roommate, one of the problems I faced was maintaining a relationship with a brother who was seventeen years younger than I. Often I would have lots of things to share with my mother and younger sister, but I found no common ground to share with my brother. His interests were vastly different, but I wanted to relate to him in some way. One day I hit on an idea that would enable us to spend time together. I arranged with my mother a day when I could take him to a special place alone. Then I told him I was going to "kidnap" him on that day and to be prepared to go with certain items, such as a lunch or jacket. It turned out to be a big hit! We went to the zoo and had a neat time. I found that he had many interests and feelings to share that I never knew he had.

We have continued these "kidnappings" periodically for the past four years. Our relationship has grown deeper. I have since married, and he has readily accepted my husband. In fact, they are the best of friends and share many interests. My husband and I plan to continue to spend special times with him at intervals.

Cozy Dinner

I am a single adult, but I live close to my mother, father, and thirteen-year-old sister. Even though I live in a small studio apartment, I make sure they come over often for dinners they especially like. It's fun eating at a card table and laughing about crowded conditions. Since I don't have a

TV, we play games and listen to music. I've also had many fun times having my younger sister over. They love this special treatment.

Grandma's Veto Power

When vacation time came, each of us children submitted requests for activities while at Grandma's, with the understanding that Grandma had veto power. Our requests were really simple ones: go fishing in the pond, color eggs, ride the tractor, swing on Greatgrandma's gate, and so forth. And Grandma rarely used her veto power.

Family Potluck

With four married children and two still at home, we needed a time for the family to continue in a spirit of togetherness. To keep us together on a regular basis, once a month we have a potluck dinner, when we visit, play games, get to know the grandchildren better, and keep up with what is happening in each family. It keeps our extended family caring for one another.

14

Happy Family Memories

And it shall come to pass, when your children shall say unto you, What mean ye by this service? That ye shall say, It is the sacrifice of the Lord's passover, who passed over the houses of the children of Israel in Egypt, when he smote the Egyptians, and delivered our houses. And the people bowed the head and worshipped.

Exodus 12:26, 27

Security Notes

One of the things that meant the most to me as a child was something my mother did to show me she considered me special and was proud of me. Whenever she attended PTA meetings or went to school for teacher conferences, the next day, I would find a note in my desk, which would read something like this:

Dear Alice,
We're proud of your schoolwork. Your teacher says good things about you. We think you are a very special girl. We love you.

Mother

I shall never forget those notes or the love and security I felt after reading them. I learned to love teacher-parent-conference days, and always opened my desk eagerly the next day, to find my note. I found myself trying extra hard each day in school, to show my love in return and to give my parents reason to be proud of me.

Both Kisses

When I was small and my father would come home from work, my mother would hold me up and we'd both kiss Daddy at the same time. We called it Both Kisses. I have started to do this in our home, and it has become a joyous, happy time of sharing when my husband comes home. Even though it's only a small thing, it really brings us close together.

Know What?

When Barbara Jo was just beginning to talk, we started our Know What? game. It wasn't long until she really understood what it was all about. I would say, "Barbara Jo, you know what?" She'd reply, "No." Then I'd go on to say, "I love you." Now it's a fun thing, because she will initiate: "Mommy, you know what?" Or, if I say it now, sometimes she'll reply, "Yes. You love me!"

Super Sue

Susan's Daddy nicknamed her Super Sue. She loved her new name, and it became a way for her daddy to communicate his love. Her older brother asked why he didn't have a "neat" name, too, so his daddy and I sat down and decided on a special name for him: Tommy Terrific. We wrote the

names on large signs and placed them on their bedroom
doors. We feel using these names at special times was a
means of drawing our family together in love.

I-Love-You Parties

We have several spontaneous parties throughout the year.
The idea first began when our eight-year-old son, Brian,
suggested that he would like to get a gift for everyone and
give them out that evening at dinner. Brian's idea seemed
like a good opportunity to encourage him to express love
and kindness for others—particularly to his younger sister,
to whom he sometimes expresses other than love and kindness! So I said, "Fine."

After discussing his plans with me, I realized that he
needed a cake made by Mother for his party. We ran over to
the store, and he purchased three small but meaningful gifts
with his allowance money. I did everything possible to make
the meal special—fresh tablecloth, candles, flowers. Brian
took charge; he handed out his gifts and said, "I love you" to
each of us.

It was such an enjoyable experience that we have each
planned our own I-Love-You parties. None has required
lots of effort; in fact, the simpler the better. We now sing a
little family song at each party, too. We all look forward to
these special times together and appreciate the refreshing
experience of restating our love for one another.

A Day as an Only Child

Occasionally I try to give to each child the fun of being an
only child for a day. One day this week, our youngest (nine)

had a free day from school because of a teachers' workday. We went to the ceramic shop, where he chose a piece to work on for a Christmas gift for his teacher. We had lunch out—just the two of us. Since he is the youngest, I like to expose him to babies once in a while, so we visited two new babies and their mothers. We bought a paint set and cut open a brown paper bag for a large mural and painted together. It was a fun, special day for both of us.

Just-Because Presents

When courting me, my husband would bring one single rose as a Just-Because Present—"Just because I love you!" I wanted this thoughtful tradition to continue, so we give Just-Because Presents: a love letter in a lunch or on a bed; a special, longed-for item earlier than birthday or Christmas; a telephone call to Grandma for one child alone to share. As a family, we look for opportunities to save for and share Just-Because Presents. Sharing is hard for children, but when Dad and Mom invest themselves in the project, the children learn by example and also experience the joy of giving and how to give a gracious thank-you.

Hero-of-the-Day Award

We have a Hero-of-the-Day award. Anyone in the family may give it to any other member. If little brother helps his sister do dishes, she notifies the family that little brother is her Hero-of-the-Day. The whole family then gives attention to the hero and praises him that day.

PART 5

HOW WE PRESERVED
OUR MEMORIES

15

Happy Memories Preserved

*I will cause Thy name to be remembered in all generations;
Therefore the peoples will give Thee thanks forever and ever.*
Psalms 45:17 NAS

This Is Your Life Scrapbook

We make a *This Is Your Life* scrapbook for each member in the family and present it on a special birthday. We cut words or sayings from books or magazines, to use next to:

- Pictures or bits of fabric of 4-H projects
- School-paper news
- A poem written by the child
- Pictures of favorite foods
- A heart's desire (such as a kitten)
- Photos of all pets of childhood days
- Vacations (with a map as a backdrop on the page under photos)
- Shells
- Leaves
- School papers with top grades, stars, or remarks
- Report cards
- Pictures and brochure of camp
- Pen-pal letters full of news and love

- A birthday decoration
- Party invitations
- Swatches of hair, with ribbons next to pictures of hairstyles of childhood
- Cards with love notes of past holidays.

What fun when each receives this special *This Is Your Life* scrapbook full of happy memories!

Bedtime Togetherness

My husband is a youth pastor and sometimes gone evenings, but the evenings he is home, we both spend time together with our three- and five-year-olds before they go to bed. My husband plays his guitar, while we sing (each takes a turn choosing a song). Then we talk, letting the boys choose the topics. At least once a month, we tape these discussions (unknown to the boys), and we're keeping the cassettes to preserve the memories.

Some discussions have been: why some children don't have parents; how to get the fishbowl to heaven without spilling the water; what was the boys' favorite activity of the day; why Aunt Mary and Uncle Jim don't love Jesus, and is Jesus sad because of that?

Mom's Letters

In my later teen years, I became a very stubborn young lady. I wouldn't let Mother talk things out with me, so Mom started writing me letters. Her letters were kind and calm, and I was able to accept her ideas better this way. I would sit down, take my time in reading it, and see her point. Then I could answer her letter and she could do the same with my letter. This became very special for us, because we were not only able to handle some sticky problems together this way, but I also got such special letters from Mom. Many times Mom would write me a poem and leave it on my dresser, for me to find the next day. Our solution to those challenging teen years was our letters. Today I cherish them!

Christmas "I Love Yous"

For Christmas Eve, each member of the family (now ages nineteen, seventeen, thirteen, six) writes a note to each other family member, beginning, "I love you because . . . ." We shared these notes during our Christmas Eve Fellowship and fun time. It is a very positive experience for all. The comments have changed greatly through the years. For instance, this year our seventeen-year-old daughter wrote, "Mom, I love you because you listen to explanations and reasons." When we first began this many years ago, it was especially difficult for my husband to put this into writing, although he expresses love in action every day. He has grown tremendously through the years in expressing himself with words. I have encouraged each one to keep the notes each year, putting them in their "treasure box" or scrapbook.

First Day of School

By taking pictures on the first day of school every September, I have a yearly picture of each child in his favorite outfit, showing colors, hairstyles, and his growth at that stage of his life. In looking back, the kids love it, and Mom's memories are keener, too.

Grandma's Box

When our mother-in-law passed away, my sister-in-law and I were trying to decide what to do with her meager worldly goods. She didn't really have anything that was of great monetary value, but there was a lot of sentiment wrapped up in her possessions. However, neither my sister-in-law nor I had room in our homes for some of her dishes, linens, jewelry, and other whatnots. Finally, we decided to make a special box for each of the grandchildren to open on his or her seventeenth birthday. We divided the different types of items up as evenly as possible and simply stored the boxes and picked one at random on each child's seventeenth birthday, marking one box for the only grandson.

After we all sing "Happy Birthday," the teenager very carefully opens his or her special box, slowly takes out each item, and passes it around the table. There are a lot of memories shared, as we each recall when Grandma used this item or that. We made this decision before the nostalgia craze hit, and we never anticipated the intense delight each child would have with the old items. Just this year, my niece was absolutely delighted to find an antique stickpin in her box. Each teenager looks forward eagerly to his seventeenth birthday, when Grandma's Box makes them feel very special.

Memory Quilt

Sixteen years ago, a little girl blessed our home. I was delighted, of course, and being fond of sewing, I was especially happy to have a daughter. I have saved material from everything I ever made for her and plan to give her a quilt made from years of memories, for her wedding. With each piece I attach a note: "Birthday-party dress, three-years-old," or, "Christmas, 1979," and so forth. I have such joy, cutting this material in the old "flat-iron" pattern, tucking away the pieces, and planning in years to come to sew them together.

I shed a few tears when I think of giving her the quilt, because it ends a period of time that she radiated so much sunshine under our roof. Even though the children are off my lap, they are never off my heart. This is one way I plan to show my daughter what a joy she has been to us through the years.

My Own Photo Album

As a family, we take many snapshots, most of which go into a large, family photo album. Realizing how much the children enjoy having things of their own, we purchased photo albums for each child. Then we went through all our extra pictures, and the children selected some for their own books. We especially included pictures of that person whose book it is. We all work together on putting the pictures in. Included are baby pictures, birthday parties, school class pictures, and so forth. The children are each proud of their book, often going to get it from their room to just sit and look at it themselves or to share it with a playmate or Grandma. I think it helps them feel how special they are.

Life-Story Book

As each of our three children turned sixteen, my husband and I prepared a photo album that was their life story up to that time. On the first page was a letter we composed together, expressing our love and joy during these sixteen years. Following this, we add our wedding picture, pictures of grandmas and grandpas and other relatives, and then pictures of the child from birth.

We include pictures of them at the ages they were when we lived in each of our homes. There were also pictures of those homes, because there were memories from each place. Then there were lots of pictures of family camping and vacation times together. One page included each year's school picture, and last of all, some very special school papers I had saved from kindergarten and the early grades. This last section especially was both a treat and a surprise. These albums have been a good thing for their self-worth. Each one eagerly looked forward to getting his book as he turned sixteen.

Did I Write That Way?

When my children were small and were bringing home all kinds of work papers from school, I remembered that I had none of these saved from my school days. We chose a place to put the things they wanted to keep. When the school year was over and there was spare time in the summer, we went through all we had saved, choosing the ones with special significance, and put them into a scrapbook. When the children became old enough to want to keep their own scrapbooks, the books were given to them, to keep and to continue adding to. These have become a source of joy to both children, who are now in college, and I'm sure they will be a treasure of happy memories for years to come.

This Is the Day

My father has such a happy, contented disposition. He passed this on to our family by joyfully quoting to us, at the beginning of the day, "This is the day which the Lord hath made; we will rejoice and be glad in it" (Psalms 118:24). We wanted to continue this daily reminder in our home, so we embroidered a sampler for the wall, bearing these words. We also sing together, as a family, the popular chorus, "This is the day which the Lord hath made." This has become "our song" and "our motto."

Recording of Family Worship

I am one of seven children, so there wasn't always time for individual attention, but Mom and Dad did take time to teach us about the love of God and make Him a part of our lives. They would gather us together every night for what we called Family Worship, where we would sing, memorize verses and the books of the Bible, and pray together. Sometimes they made tape recordings of us. Now it's really something, to go back and hear ourselves—little three-year-olds on up—saying Bible verses and singing. My parents gave up a lot for us seven kids and for the work they did for the Lord. They are very special people.

Summer Memory Book

This summer, as a family, we made a book recording things we did during the summer. We started by writing goals for each member.

- Sally (six years old): Keep room clean. Help with house chores. Establish regular quiet times with the Lord.
- Daddy: New goals at work. Quality time with family. Learn and teach family more about faith.
- Mother: Regular quiet times. Prepare for birth of child (due end of summer). Spend time with Sally, especially teaching her to cook.

Each Monday at family night, we wrote down what we had done each day of that previous week. Then each person drew a picture to illustrate some event of the past week. Very special events received extra-special pictures and explanations. The result? We have a precious record of some very important, monumental events that took place. Sally lost her first tooth! Grandpa Olson left us to be with the Lord. And Jesus gave us a new baby sister!

P.S. This was also helpful for those "What did I do this summer" reports, when Sally started school again.

Is That My Voice?

We tape our children's voices at various ages. Sometimes we plan an interview program, asking them questions about their interests at this stage in their lives. At other times, unknown to the children, we tape the conversation around the dinner table. They love to listen to tapes of when they were first learning to talk, and it's a precious thing for us to keep with our memories.

Something-New Notebook

I keep a notebook of something new our twenty-month-old son does each day. It serves as a point of reference for communication with my husband, when he comes home from work, so he might also enjoy his child's growth. I also believe it will help our child's self-concept, as we point out the progress he makes each day. And it will be the beginning of a memory book that will be more precious as the years go by.

Home-Worship Tapes

Our family plans a special home service at the religious holidays. Each child takes his turn planning either the whole service or a part, depending on his age. Even the youngest can sing or recite a Sunday-school verse. A bulletin or order of worship is made up by the child in charge. These are handmade and lovingly designed with special artwork, according to that one's abilities. Each person has his own copy. We have taped some of these worship times together. Listening to these, years later, has been a great source of enjoyment that binds the family together with happy memories. The bulletins the children made have been saved and treasured.

Summer camping gives occasions for special worship services out-of-doors, with spectacular scenery as our cathedral of God. We all agree that these holiday services have brought us closer to God and closer to one another in a wonderful way.

Journal of Gratefulness

About six months ago, my husband initiated our Journal of Gratefulness to God. He had me buy a five-year diary. Once a week, for our family devotion time, we make entries of what special ways God has shown His hand toward us that past week—either specific answers to prayer or some situation that was God's obvious doing. Occasionally we look back through parts of it and are encouraged in our faith and reminded to thank God for what He has done. It also helps us to become aware of things that are important to others in the family. Each of us has enjoyed this practice, and we expect it to continue to build our faith and thankfulness for years to come.

Diary of a Mother-to-Be

I kept a personal diary during my time as a mother-to-be, writing of the joys and expectations I had in having this baby. Each diary will be presented to the child, someday. This is one way I hope to communicate to each one how much he or she was longed for and loved from the very beginning.

Epilogue

I vividly remember, as we were going home from church one Sunday evening when I was quite young, Mother very thoughtfully said, "I do hope that if anyone ever challenges you to deny your faith, you will stand for the Lord, whatever the cost. I am praying that you will have the grace to do that."

This was not the only time she said that or something similar. It was written indelibly upon my mind. Her loving, prayerful, concerned words did not implant fear in me, but courage, challenge, direction, and a goal: to stand for Jesus, whatever the cost.

This precious memory was written upon my mind even before I knew Jesus Christ personally and had committed my life to Him. In fact, as a young teenager, I recall a time when a group of girls were planning an afternoon together. They suggested we do something that my conscience would not allow me to do. I said, "I'm sorry, I cannot do that. You all go ahead, and I'll just meet you later." Even though my mother was not there and would never realize that I had refused to be part of that activity, which was questionable to my young conscience, the memory of the goal she implanted was a real strength to me in that situation. I'm confident this also contributed to my committing my life to Jesus Christ several years later.

When I was fifteen years old, I made a definite transaction, receiving Jesus Christ to be my personal Savior and the Lord of my life.

And this is the record, that God hath given to us eternal life, and this life is in his Son. He that hath the Son hath life; and he that hath not the Son of God hath not life. These things have I written unto you that believe on the name of the Son of God; that ye may know that ye have eternal life, and that ye may believe on the name of the Son of God.

1 John 5:11–13

Have you, my dear reader, made this kind of commitment? If not, I urge you to do so. This then will become for you the most significant happy memory, the fullness of which can only be realized in eternity.

If you are a parent, one of your prayer goals and life goals should be to do what you can to give your child the gift of this most precious memory—commitment of his or her life to Jesus Christ as Savior and Lord. The commitment will be his, but you can do much to lay a foundation for it by building a good relationship with him, living an example before him, praying for him, and at proper times giving encouragement and direction in the Way.

The ideas shared in this valuable little volume can help you build a meaningful relationship with your children as you build happy memories for them. This good relationship will, in turn, provide a foundation for a positive response to the example of your godly life and give strength and validity to the words you speak and the ideals you hold.